For L and G
"Fly high"
—H. F.

Para L y G
"Fly high"
—H. F.

This edition published by Parragon Books Ltd in 2014 and distributed by
Edición publicada por Parragon Books Ltd en 2014 y distribuida por

Parragon Inc.
440 Park Avenue South, 13th Floor
New York, NY 10016
www.parragon.com

Edited by Laura Baker
Designed by Ailsa Cullen

Editado por Laura Baker
Diseño de Ailsa Cullen

Traducción del inglés: Sara Chiné Segura para LocTeam, Barcelona

Printed in China
Impreso en China

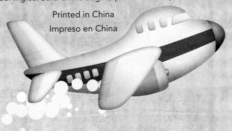

Away
in my airplane

Volando
en mi avioneta

Written by Margaret Wise Brown

Illustrated by Henry Fisher

Texto de Margaret Wise Brown

Ilustraciones de Henry Fisher

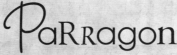

PaRragon

Bath • New York • Singapore • Hong Kong • Cologne • Delhi
Melbourne • Amsterdam • Johannesburg • Shenzhen

Riding along in
my airplane,

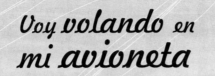

Voy *volando* en
mi *avioneta*

Over the clouds and through the rain.

haciendo más de una pirueta.

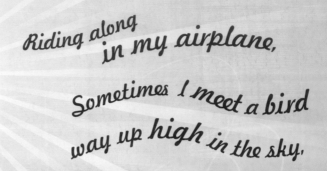

Riding along
in my airplane,

Sometimes I meet a bird
way up high in the sky,

Voy volando
en mi avioneta,
por la noche y por el día.

Flying almost as fast as I fly—
But not as high!

y a los pájaros que me encuentro,
los saludo muy contento.

Riding along
in my airplane,

Voy volando
por la ciudad

Out of the sunlight and

y aunque haga sol o llueva

into the rain

mi avioneta se eleva.

Then out of the clouds
and SUN again,

Atravieso las nubes sin miedo
y antes de caer al suelo

Riding along in my airplane!

¡levanto el vuelo!

Down below the people go,
very small and very slow.

La gente va de paseo
sin saber que yo los veo.

They look like bugs and ants and flies—
I wonder if they realize
What they **look** like to my eyes.

Desde aquí arriba
hormiguitas parecen,
pero si me acerco crecen.

Riding along in my airplane,

Voy volando en mi avioneta...

I **wave** to the sun,

bajo el **radiante** sol

Then, with a roar of my motors that drowns me out,

El rugido del motor ahoga mi grito,

I **dash** straight up in the air

And wheel about.

volar es mi pasatiempo favorito.

I *plunge* through the sunlight,

Hacia el sol voy volando en mi avioneta

I hurl through the *rain*,

y de vez en cuando
hago alguna **pirueta**.

Then I glide
down to the earth
in my airplane.

Ya es la hora,
voy bajando,
mi familia me está esperando.

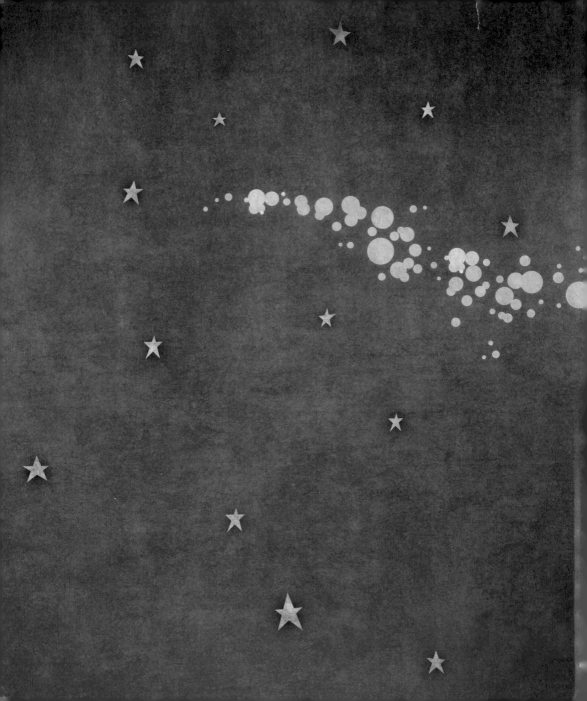